AMERICAN JESUS

POEMS
BY
RICHARD VARGAS

TIA CHUCHA PRESS
LOS ANGELES

I would like to thank the editors of these publications for previously publishing the following, sometimes in a different version:

Used with permission of copyright holder *Bilingual Review / Editorial Bilingue:*
   "Driving to O'Hare," "For Aunt Connie... With Love" first published in *Bilingual Review,*
   Vol. 24, No. 3, Arizona State University, Tempe, AZ.
Breakast All Day (BAD) *"9 Men, 25 Women, 14 Children, One Infant," "Whimper"*
Chiron Review *"Racism 101"*
Main Street Rag *"Truer Words," "Soulmate," "Another Nature Poem," "Five Hundred,"*
   "Army Poem III & IV"
Princeton Arts Review *"On The Outside"*
Rattle *"And Yet, Another Nature Poem"*
Rockhurst Review *"How I Became He-Weeps-Fire"*
The Rockford Review *"American Jesus," "It's a Living II"*
Vampire's Ball *"It Happens to the Best of Us"*
Willow Review *"Driving to Platteville"*
Wormwood Review *"I Got Them Dirty Underwear Blues," "The Job, a Swing Shift Lament,"*
   "What Does it Mean?"
Xispas.com *"Spider-Man in Albuquerque"*

ISBN 978-882688-34-0
Book Design: Jane Brunette
Front and Back Cover Photo: Mark Bond

PUBLISHED BY:
Tia Chucha Press
A Project of Tia Chucha's Centro Cultural
PO Box 328
San Fernando, CA 91341
www.tiachucha.com

DISTRIBUTED BY:
Northwestern University Press
Chicago Distribution Center
11030 South Langley Avenue
Chicago, IL 60628

Tia Chucha Press is supported by the National Endowment for the Arts and operating funds from Tia Chucha's Centro Cultural. Tia Chucha's Café & Centro Cultural have received support from Los Angeles County Arts Commission, the Los Angeles Department of Cultural Affairs, Los Angeles Community Redevelopment Agency, Trill Hill Foundation, Panta Rhea Foundation, the Center for Cultural Innovation, the Middleton Foundation, Not Just Us Foundation, the Liberty Hill Foundation, Youth Can Service, Toyota Sales, Solidago Foundation, and other grants and donors including Bruce Springsteen, John Densmore, Dan Attias, Dave Marsh, David Sandoval, Denise Chávez and John Randall of the Border Book Festival, Luis & Trini Rodríguez, and others.

for
Ed Field
poet/mentor/friend

TABLE OF CONTENTS

"But why should we hear about body bags, and deaths, and how many, what day it's gonna happen, and how many this or what do you suppose? Or, I mean, it's, it's not relevant. So why should I waste my beautiful mind on something like that?"

BARBARA BUSH
ON "GOOD MORNING AMERICA,"
MARCH 18, 2003

he walked away from the city
and the bright lights
found a town where a tall
building is considered
anything over two stories
he doesn't miss the super
hero gig
all the bad guys now wear
suits and class rings from
ivy league schools
where's the fun in that?

the closest he came to
helping someone in distress
in his new city was the time
two cops chased a homeless
man away from patio seating at
one of the trendy restaurants
in Nob Hill

he caught up with the guy
gave him a couple of bucks
felt good about it
better than any ass whipping
he ever had to dish out to the
freak of the week

he misses his girl and
the dimple in her wicked
smile when he used to tie
her up with his webbing
practicing various japanese
S&M knots

Maryjane married rich
lives in northern Calif
raises championship horses
hosts republican fundraisers
where the highlight of the
evening is when the band
plays "Tie a Yellow Ribbon..."
and the wealthy get up
to shake their booty

on hot summer nights
he latches on to the top
of a city bus
rides up and down
Central Ave from
the Sandia Mts all
the way downtown

counts a star in the desert
sky for every regret he
ever had and then counts
another one for everytime
he felt like the luckiest
man alive

SOULMATE

the second time we met
at Sonny's bar she was
telling me about the short
stories of Paul Bowles
and how some of them
made her feel high

she said she was going
home to get the book
for me and i'm thinking
"yeah, right..."
but 15 minutes later
she walks back in
puts the book in front
of me on the bar
orders another beer

later
the drunk jailbird
from Arizona who
had been bumming
drinks all night
leans over and asks
if she'd like to go
make out in the
parking lot

the great ones never
miss an opening and i
knew she was something
special when
shaking her head no
she looks at me and
says "i'd rather have
my nipples shaved off
with a cheese grater..."

POOL

many a quarter is lost
until one day at the table
everything comes together
a world defined on dingy
green felt in a smoke hazed
room and everyone is watching
as you seize it
dissect it with some sort of primeval
geometry imbedded in your genes
you sense the elation of those around you
at the sight of a man grasping
control of his destiny for the 1st time
since who-knows-when
the 8 ball gracefully sinking out
of sight ending the game too soon
like a quick and unexpected sunset on one of
those rare days when everything goes right

another quarter goes down
everyone agreeing it's such a small price to pay

SUCCESS... FOR LYNYRD SKYNYRD

sitting in a bar after work
sipping a beer and contemplating the
strange turn my life has taken

everything is going my way
editors no longer send me
one word rejection slips
got promoted at my job
got a date next week
with a woman who has been
the leading lady in my dreams for
the last three months

when out of nowhere the jukebox
comes on with a song by one of my
favorite bands
their last plane ride together
left them scattered all over
the countryside like so many
pieces of the Colonel's chicken
tossed out the window
of a speeding r.v.

finishing my beer
i get up to leave and
outside the evening rain
has transformed the street's
blacktop surface into a slick
stretch of relocated runway

and while still remembering you
i fasten my seatbelt

hope for the best

KNOW THE FEELING?

don't say you never
know what it's like
to have so much
love inside and
nowhere to put it

so much trying
to get out it
makes you cry
while staring into
the monitor on your desk
riding the bus downtown
or eating eggs and bacon
in your favorite diner
surrounded by people
all feeling just like you do
but no one willing to make
the first move

until one day
while watching tv
or taking a nap on the couch
you double over
as it punches its way out
rips open your beer belly
like a baby alien
but now it's changed
mutated into something else
innocent and vicious
starved for affection
it begins to feed and grow

your last thought
before succumbing to
the shock and the pain
is of the crazy world
we live in and how
it finally

all makes sense

the greatest compliment
i ever got was from Cecil Wall
a combat vet from Korea and
two tours in Nam
he was black as
midnight without the moon
bald head slick
like a pair of his spit
shined boots
his beer keg chest
decorated with battle scars
permanent reminders of
beating the odds when it
counted the most

you couldn't miss the nasty
one on his neck and he would
only tell you once about being
paralyzed on his back
the only sounds he could hear
were charlie's footsteps moving
through the elephant grass and
the gurgling of blood
spurting from his throat
when out of nowhere a
buddy picked him up
slung him over and double-
timed their asses outta
harm's way just like in
the movies but then again
where do you think they
get this stuff?

and he would tell you about
coming home
how good it felt to be back
even if the welcome of a grateful
nation was out of the question
then the riots in Detroit
erupted and his unit was
deployed to patrol the streets
where he was shot at by his
own people and i'll never forget
how he stared off into space
said in a tone cold as death
"fuck it... it was like being back
in Nam, and we acted accordingly..."
then he would pick up his
CC&7 and down it with
one gulp

it was during one such episode
as we were drinking back at
my place
a farewell of sorts as my reporting
date for OCS drew near
First Sergeant Wall finished
his drink then held out his
empty glass
i mixed him another as he started
talking about leaders and assholes
and the fine line that separates
the two

then he said it
words i will carry with me
until i breathe my last
"Corporal Vahhhgus, i'd
follow you into battle.
i know i'd be alright with you..."

ask yourself how many times
in a life does a man turn to
you proclaiming his blind
trust in your judgement when
the worst kind of shit
hits the biggest fan
pulls his bloody heart from
his chest and puts it in your
hands for safekeeping

for most of us
it will never happen
but if it does
handle the moment
with respect and care

to be considered
a gift
a delicate
silence
to be broken
only

by the sound
of clinking ice

It Happens to the Best of Us

she's turning pale
whiter than a sheet in a Chlorox commercial
refuses to come out during the day
has stopped wearing underwear
under long clingy gowns
revealing curves and crevices
you still long to kiss
sensing she desperately wants
to pull you close you reach
for her only to notice her
inner struggle to keep you
at arm's length
"no... no! i can't! i still love you..."
as she opens the door to her apt
sends you home to another
cold shower or mary palm
and her five sisters

lately
you've caught her staring
at your neck
dark eyes transfixed
with hunger and lust
saliva drips from the corner
of her mouth as the tip of
a tongue red as passion
fruit barely parts her lips

on the day you're wondering
why she's taken down
all her mirrors including the
one on the medicine cabinet
she calls you on the phone to say
she can't see you anymore
weeps as she says it's over

"but babe, we can work it out..."
"no! you must stay away
for your own good... promise!"
she hangs up and when you
drop by after work her place
is empty with no forwarding
address to be found

and just like that
she's walked out of your
life forever leaving you to
pick up the pieces
you want to join the marines
leave the country
swipe razor blades
across both wrists
but time does heal all
wounds until she only
haunts your sleep and
the memories about
the good times you both
shared begin to fade
like old dreams

a year later you're standing in line
with your new girl waiting to get in
for the Rolling Stones farewell concert
as you check out the stretch limos
pulling up and the VIPs using the
special entrance she steps out of one
glowing translucent like a statue
chiseled from polar ice
she's wearing a designer gown
fitting like a second skin
that would set you back
two months pay
her escort is just as cold
looks like a model you saw

in Esquire magazine
except this guy
drips testosterone
and even though he's
wearing shades his chilling
smile reminds you of a
great white rising to the
surface where you float
on your board waiting
for the next wave
then you realize
he's staring right
at you

and somehow
deep inside
you know
things have
turned out
for the best

FIVE HUNDRED

the news made it sound
like something to get
excited about

we tend to think of
the number as a milestone
Barry Bonds hitting home runs
a sitcom still on the air
a fast food conglomerate
opening one more drive-thru

but i imagine planes
landing and expelling
dark military issue coffins
from their deep hollow
bellies
a detail of soldiers
greeting them one by one
the white gloves they wear
on their hands making it
easy to follow as they
surrender the crisp motion
required for a proper
salute

they may not let us
see them arriving
cold and alone
but there is a stench
in the air
and no matter
how many times
we bathe

it won't wash off

9 MEN, 25 WOMEN, 14 CHILDREN, ONE INFANT

it's the day after Jesus' birthday
the devout have come to see
how much they can save on marked
down Christmas cards and wrapping paper
these post-holiday locusts looking
for the crumbs they missed

the picture in today's
paper shows the coffins lined up
mourners in the Chiapas sun
beating their breasts
9 men, 25 women, 14 children, one infant
greeted with bullets and machetes on their
way to worship a complacent god

"how much are these cards with the discount?"
but i don't answer
ignore this american cow
with too much makeup and a cheap dye job
instead i hear the sound of a mountain
breeze rustling trees
or is it the wheeze of a sucking
chest wound

"i need to exchange this, do i have
to get in that long line?"
no you don't
you can come with me and walk along
this stream of fresh water
cool and crisp
ponder its bubbling song
washing over ancient rocks
or is that wet noise
a child choking on its own blood

"how long is this sale going to last?"
as long as human lives
can be bought and sold
traded and smuggled
stomped on and swept under the rug
in a world where precious metals
and shiny rocks outweigh your worth
or mine

finally i answer feeling the tears
forming in the corners of my eyes
"these cards were originally priced at $10.50,
and with the sale price you save $5.25."
the customer is happy
corporate is happy
America is happy
everyone is happy except

9 men, 25 women, 14 children,
and one infant

RECONQUEST

his ghost walks the vacant aisles late at night
eating a bag of doritos and drinking
a coke he pauses in sporting goods
admires the hunting knives under the
glass case and remembers how it felt
to hold a man's warm beating
heart in his hand

now
his sons have swapped
jaguar skins and quetzal feathers
for retail blue
their new war cry
stenciled on their backs

his daughters are sacrificed
their corpses found randomly
in the desert
tortured burned and mutilated
tributes to the new gods of
free trade and open markets

he stands amid the cheap
merchandise as outside
blue plastic bags
cling to nearby
fences waving
in the wind like
a new national flag

unlike the benevolent feathered serpent
it has replaced
this one is coiled tight
as it takes its place in the shadow

of the great pyramid
ready to strike without warning

here to stay
for a long
long time

WATCHING MY OLD MAN KICK SOMEONE'S ASS

i was three maybe four
looked out the screen door
there he was across the street
people were standing in a circle
he and another man were in the middle
my old man must have been in his early 20s
lean hard and mean
fresh out of the 82nd airborne
the other guy was soft
a pendejo who never left the block
my dad was throwing his shit
left and right
his opponent was backing up into
the crowd losing his footing
but afraid to take his eyes off
the crazy cholo coming at him
it was over before it really started
my old man victorious and cocky
i remember he looked from
across the street
saw me standing in the doorway
our eyes met and i knew he had
just shown me something important
i took a mental snapshot
so i'd always carry
the moment with me

now
when i want to strike out
unleash the blow we all
have within us
i write a poem

and i know
he would
approve

END-OF-TIMES SEX

first
we'll be freaked
struggle with the necessities
food water shelter
the cost of a scarce roll
of our favorite toilet paper
will make the coin we pay
for a gallon of gas look like
pocket change
but after the great adaptation
after we find our groove
as our species always does
our attention will turn to
the more important things

by the light of a precious
candle we'll remember the
art of undressing each other
the tease of a zipper pulled
oh so slow
the thrill of balancing her calf
in one hand while sucking her
little toe gently like
a ripe and delicate grape
our tongues will go places
they almost forgot
purring like cats will
become a natural response
as naked skin glides
across naked skin

then
taking a break between the warm sheets
tearing open a package of oreos
from our emergency disaster stash
feeding them to each other

discovering the joy of taking turns
licking the crumbs off our partner's backside
we'll wonder aloud what the hell we were
supposed to be afraid of
and why?

we were taking a break between clutches
in the Motel 6 darkness,
waiting for our second wind.
when, for no reason at all, she started.
1st, i heard about the episode with a perfect stranger
in San Diego, a hitchhiker who turned her on
to some acid, and left her in the backseat of her car
at a local drive-in, her panties on backwards.
then, there was the middle-aged, recently divorced
business executive who kept falling asleep
despite the romantic fireplace setting and
a hundred and twenty dollar a night view
of the beach.
this led to her 1st time, a high school jock
who came in three seconds and asked her if she
was alright.
the clincher, though, was the one night stand who led
her to believe that he was single, and while wrestling
between the sheets at his place, what should her feet
get tangled in except for a pair of his wife's dirty
underwear.

i sat up, wondered what she would say about me,
the poet with a pecker shrinking like an
elongated balloon with a slow leak.

How I Know There is a God

some people go to church on Sunday
but i always preferred the
Coliseum in downtown L.A.
my old man took me there to see
my first pro game when i was 5 yrs old
saw Fran Tarkenton and his new team
in purple beat our beloved Rams
i learned new four lettered words that day
it was imbedded into my young
developing male consciousness
that ol' Fran was a prick
an opinion i've never been
able to shake

through the decades i went there often
becoming one with the concession stands
the sweet aroma of foot long hot dogs
and cold beer topped with foam
the scalpers brazenly holding tickets
in the air to get my attention
the hundred charcoal fires burning
in the parking lot as gray smoke drifted
overhead and the smells of bar-b-que
and carne asada hung heavy in the
hot September air like a working man's
incense

the Coliseum is sacred ground, man
sacred

the last NFL team to call it home
were the Raiders
a team that used to be able to win
when the odds were stacked against them
but since their last Super Bowl

victory in '83 have hit hard times
stayed in pause mode while the
rest of the league hit fast forward
but i love them anyway
always went to a game feeling
they would finally awaken and prevail

on this particular gameday
they were up to their usual
as they fumbled
got penalized
and gave the other team enough
breaks to win the game just
for showing up

making matters worse
i had a couple of obnoxious drunks
sitting in front of me wearing
Chicago Bears' jerseys who were
providing biting commentary
taunting the hometown fans on their
own turf and breaking up into hysterics
when the Raider QB threw a pass
end over end that fell like a block
of concrete 10 yds. short of the
intended target
then they said they came on a bus
outta Vegas and had a shit-wad of
dough bet against my team and afterwards
they would be chugging cold ones all the
way back to collect their winnings

during the last 10 minutes of the game
while i contemplated making a dash
for the car and beating the traffic
this old guy gets up at the end of the
row of seats in front of me and stumbles
doing a great Dean Martin imitation

the two Bears fans had to stand
so the guy could pass
as he ascended the steps to
the exit tunnel weaving back and forth
my tormentors took a double take
and one said to the other
"holy shit, did you see who that was?
that was our bus driver... we're fucked!"

as they ran up the stairs to check on
the guy who was supposed to get
them home safe and sound
i took a long swallow from my
warm beer and decided to watch
the end of the game

smiled to myself
as i realized this was better
than a burning bush

and 10 times more convincing

THIS REALLY HAPPENED

i was at this drive-in movie watching
this flick and holding back from going to
the john for at least a 1/2 hour because i
didn't want to miss any good parts.

(like the scene where this broad's eyes
get poked out by a big black bird, and she
stumbles onto the highway and gets pulverized
by this whining diesel...actually showed it
in slow motion.)

finally, when there seemed to be a lull
in the action, i decided to make a break for it.
as i grabbed the door handle, a voice interrupted
the movie and said,
"peter schmuck, please come to the snack bar,
peter schmuck, please come to the snack bar."

i heard the couple parked next to me giggle,
and someone said, "who the fuck is peter schmuck?"

well, what would you have done?
i waited another fifteen minutes.

ARMY POEM II

Joe the XO graduated from
West Point but you'd never
know it because he was
top heavy for an infantry
officer with a W.C. Fields
nose and surfer blonde hair
looked like a young Santa
minus the beard

when training in the field
after the mess tent was
situated and the fueling
schedule for the company's
vehicles was set he always
found the nearest fishing hole
finding the time to cast
a line or two while filling
an empty c-ration can with
dark brown tobacco juice

his favorite story was how
one night in the dark he meant
to reach for the k-y jelly but
grabbed the vicks vapo-rub instead
his depiction of how he and
the little lady started to scream
once they got going always left
us with tears in our eyes

so you can imagine my surprise
the day he pulled me aside
pointed to one of our sergeants
and said "ever notice how some
of these guys look like monkeys?"
the oblivious smile on his face

reminding me how sad i felt
the day i realized George Allen
really was blackballed from
coaching in the NFL
or when they killed off the Duke
at the end of *The Cowboys*

at the end of the day
i went back to my room
soaked in a tub of water
as hot as i could stand it
sipped a cold beer
lit a cigar

scrubbed my skin
raw
knew i wouldn't
feel clean for
a long time

For Olivia, Dying

funny
always thought i'd be there
at your side
the dutiful son holding your hand
but now it's relief i feel
half way across the country and
finally able to stand straight
as the weight slips from my shoulders

i remember well the life lessons you gave me
how to discard family relations like used candy wrappers
the ability to turn the heart into a piece of coal
how to be desperate for the good life
and give your children a deaf ear
as they cry out in the dark shadow
of a stepfather's lewd smile

i know the fear that motivates an animal
to gnaw its own leg off
run and stumble into the night
get far away as possible

now, after many years of trying to unlearn
what i can never forget
i return the favor
present a life lesson of my own
from me to you

when the pain is so unbearable
my name cursed for not showing
the respect you thought was your maternal right
remember this:

certain flowers survive the freezing kiss of December
thrive in the smothering heat of August

they can be pulled out
mowed under
spitted and shitted on

yet
when least expected
they will still rise up to the sun
and bloom

when lunch time comes around,
we head out to the parking lot,
a migratory herd of caribous looking for greener pastures.
we pull out our pipes, our papers, our smoke.
we talk about getting fucked by the bossman,
the union,
our women.
and always the new job we're going to go out looking
for tomorrow.

when we return to the warehouse,
the old guys sitting down with cups of
coffee in their hands notice our arrival,
smelling the lingering smoke and saying nothing.
these oldtimers with the thick skin of a rhino's hide
have known the pain.
they look the other way.
and in our silence
we know it's just a matter of time.

the girl on stage had the face of a young
Mayan princess, the body of a playboy centerfold.
tugging at her black bikini bottoms,
she smiled at me.
and if i'd had it to bargain with, my soul would
have been hers.

which brings to mind my 8th grade english teacher
and the time she kept me after class to discuss
something i had written. she paced back and forth
in front of my desk, looking like a conviction
crazed prosecutor warming up for the kill.
she waved my composition in front of my face
like it was a piece of prized evidence.
"this bit about looking up the girl's dress
in your math class... what does it mean?"

she caught me by surprise, and i just sat there
like a startled jackrabbit, blinded by a pair of
approaching headlights.

SCARIEST DREAM EVER

woke up
stumbled to
the bathroom
to pee
turned on light
pulled down shorts
screamed

Nike Swoosh
on the head
of my dick

REINCARNATING

people in India call me
they are paid to call me
they have names like Justin
or Megan and when i ask
they can't tell me
where they are
calling from
it's not authorized
information

but they have soft
exotic accents and
a polite tone of voice
i derive satisfaction
knowing they will
make lousy bill
collectors
they ask why i'm
not paying my Visa bill
i tell them i can't find
a decent job
they are silent
like someone trying
to tiptoe around a
minefield

they want to make it
easy for me and pre-
arrange payment
all they need is my
checking account
number and
this is how it starts

then they will want
all my sexual fantasies
and my I.Q.
my shoe size
and my favorite color
what food gives me heartburn
did i ever air guitar to a song
by Led Zepplin and if so
which one
when did i lose my virginity
and who did i vote for
in the last election
slowly i'll begin
to vanish
disappear
like the invisible man
until one day
i'll lay down at night
only to wake up
on the banks of
a mighty river
dark people with
beautiful white teeth
will pull me to the
muddy brown waters
urge me to bathe
and pray

i will say the strange names
of gods i don't know
launch delicate bouquets
of red and gold flowers
that drift slowly out of sight
feel like i had something
important to do
but can't remember
what it was

THE PASSION 2004

stripped
beaten
pulled by the rope
around his neck
he ends up posed
with his arms stretched
wide and his head hanging
low as he awaits his fate while
all around him fair skinned
soldiers from an occupying army
sent by the western world
to save him from himself
and secure his country's
natural resources
make jokes about his
dark brown penis
someone drapes Mary
Magdalene's panties
over his head to be
worn like a thorny
crown

our sons and
daughters are bored
take photos for posterity
and the internet
wearily suck on
cigarettes while
wondering when they
can go home

the only thing missing
is the rolling of dice

YOU DON'T SPEAK FOR ME, CINDY

don't speak for me
when you refuse to
accept the reasons
your son had to die

don't speak for me
when you demand
our holy roller leader
with his blacked out
military records
look you in the eye
and say once again
how he understands
your pain

don't speak for me
when the mobs try
to string you up with
red white & blue
rope and treating
you fair and balanced
means putting a
target on your back
and front

don't speak for me, Cindy
i want you to

scream

SICK CALL

the time between
them is getting shorter
the days when i can't do
it anymore
stare at a monitor for 8-10 hrs
taking calls while counting
the minutes between breaks
until the shift ends
and i walk out the door
feeling numb and frustrated
like i've been masturbating
continuously without release
remembering the countless days
of mowing
cooking
selling
loading
warehousing
supervising
delivering
servicing
cashiering
learning the arts of bullshit
and kissing ass for
a cave
a chunk of meat
a fire to keep me warm
and dry

but this is also an art onto itself
as i practice my best
George Burns imitation
my throat turning into a piece
of gravelled road
my breathing becomes labored

like a man pulling himself out of
his deathbed as i call the boss
interlace my voice with suppressed
suffering and a hint of regret
once the deed is done
i make some coffee
turn on the tv
maybe write a poem
that's been banging around
in my head
take a shower
go out for some breakfast
sometimes ride a bus downtown
catch an early matinee

it's like finding something
valuable that you thought
you'd lost

or even better
stealing it back

KONG SPEAKS #1... FOR RON KOERTGE

sometimes our fate is already set
we go along for the ride waiting
for the accident to happen

seeing her for the first time
tied up and helpless
her screams reaching high notes
i didn't think were possible
the full moon's light bouncing
off her shiny yellow hair
those perky breasts ready
to pop out of her Banana
Republic white cotton shirt
well... who could resist?
i knew she was a keeper
even when she fainted and peed
on herself upon seeing lil' Kong
standing firm and erect
begging for her soft touch

always the eternal optimist
i refused to let her go
having her in my hand beat
humping my favorite rock
back at the cave anyday
but you see where this
is going

how many times do we
walk the path of
painful uncertainty
condemn the heart to be
thrown into the air

a grenade with
the pin pulled

hoping it will be
different
this time

so the day i found myself higher
than i'd ever been
looking out over a concrete
and steel horizon
strange lines and shapes making me
realize i'd arrived at a place
where i could never belong
i asked myself
"what do i do now?"
as if on cue
i heard the distant beating
of the drums
having led me here
now calling me back

i took a long gaze upon the
city i was leaving
looked down upon the woman
never meant to return my love
dreams die hard
sometimes we die with them
but when the drums call
wherever you are
whatever you're doing
hold your head high
swallow back the regret
rising in your throat

let go
and don't
look back

KILLING MEXICANS... FOR ESEQUIEL HERNANDEZ

in this country marines
kill mexicans tending sheep
because they look like
drug dealers, terrorists
or worse, illegal landscapers

in this country laws are being passed
to wipe our culture from the land
in California they call them propositions
one of the definitions of the word is
"a request for sexual intercourse"
so i guess this means they are being polite
asking for our permission
before they screw us

in this country
they want us to speak
only english
the official language
of the done deal
the broken treaty
the limp handshake
a tv politician's promise

in this country
we are taking back
the land one minimum
wage job at a time
laughing at their
Taco Bell paranoias
and sour cream fears

they are building walls
to keep us out
but the joke's on them

we never
left

AMERICAN JESUS

leads us into the new crusades
kicks open Muslim doors
under cover of darkness
gives the frightened children
chocolate bars with wrappers
depicting the father, the son
and the half dead vice-president

he multiplies a loaf of Wonder Bread
and a couple of cans of tuna into
M-16s, tanks, and planes
drops a bomb for every man
woman and child refusing our
holy gifts of crooked democracy
and tainted freedom

his disciples spend money
that hasn't been printed yet
they urge us to be patriotic
start Christmas shopping
in June

American Jesus invites us
to the real Last Supper
and this time
the flesh
we eat
the blood
we drink
will be our
own

ARMY POEM III

the guy hated the army
but his rich old man said he couldn't
claim his share of the family fortune
unless he made something of himself
he'd been kicked out of four schools
catering to the brats of the uppercrust
so this was his last chance

during the three months of our
infantry officer basic training he caught v.d.
got arrested for pissing in public
was chased naked down the hallway
of our living quarters by someone with a knife
was thrown in jail for drunk driving
got in trouble for calling a visiting officer
from Nigeria a "darkie" at the officer's club

but the worst was the night they had us out
on maneuvers in the Georgia woods
the rain was falling so hard we wondered
why anyone would want to fight a war
while getting so wet and cold at the same time
the guys who were supposed to attack
us were smarter than we were
they never bothered to show up
so he took cover under a tree
lit up a cigarette
when lightning struck
threw him 8 ft into the air
his clothes flew off
he landed with a thud
and started running around naked
in circles as the smoke rising
from his head made him look

like a big roman candle that turned
out to be a dud

we all thought this was a message
it just wasn't meant to be
but Uncle Sam is deaf to words
like "luck" and "fate"

somewhere in Europe
he's guarding nuclear warheads

Rock n' Roll Aunt

i was only 5 or 6
but you used to
give me carte blanche
with your 45s and RCA
portable record player
when we came over to visit

in your room laid out
on your bed i'd listen to
the Everly Bros/Chubby Checker/
Bobby Rydell/Ritchie
Valens/Frankie Avalon
and the King whose sultry
voice made me want
to get up and move in
mysterious ways

you always knew the latest dances too
the watusi/mashed potato/the twist
on saturday nights you took
your turn strolling between
the other kids all swaying
in unison to the sounds of
Art Laboe's rock n' roll shows
and what would one day
be known as the eastside sound

your hair teased high
coy pink lips and
hypnotic maybelline eyes
the boys with dark skin
and slicked hair stood
in line for a chance
to dance with you

an angel from the
other side of the tracks

many moons have passed
now you're in icu
fading in and out
between cancer's
steady hunger and the
drugs they give you to
numb the pain
the miles between us
are many
but if i could be there
at your side
i'd thank you for planting the
seeds of teenage rebellion
in my tiny heart

whisper in your ear
how after all these years
that timeless question
of your youth will
finally be answered:

who
who
who wrote
the book of love?

IT'S A LIVING II

it's one of those days
the first call was a guy
in New York pissed off
cuz we're not gonna fill
his prescription for viagra
until his dr calls and answers
a few questions
upset with the delay
regarding his love-drug
he assumes the right to tell
me that i work for a real
"chickenshit outfit"
and that he hopes i get
the shaft one day soon

it goes downhill from there
as i start counting the minutes
until i can get up and walk
out at the end of my shift
leaving the stench of
another wasted day
hanging over my desk

and that's how it would
have been except for
the little old lady who called
to inquire about her
10 prescriptions and
the balance on her account
proceeding to tell me
about the 768 dollars
she gets every month
so she can only order
three medications at a time
staggering her refills

prioritizing them by
necessity and cost

she talks about the good
week she had collecting cans
got 18 extra bucks to
pay towards her bill

i hear her smile as she
tells me how getting
out and about keeps
her mind alert and her
joints from getting stiff

at the end of her call
she thanks me
tells me how we
do such a great job
she loves the service

later
i bring up the company website
our stock is 20 points higher
than it was 3 months ago

i was regretting not buying any
with my employee discount

but not now

SNAPSHOT OF LORIE... DAVIS, ILLINOIS

i drive up to my lady's
house in the country
pulling into the gravel
driveway as storm
clouds float toward
me from the west

the breeze from the advancing
rain reminds me of the last
time a smelled a baby
fresh from the bath
pure and sweet

the only sounds are the leaves
singing back to the wind
and i'm thinking how
fortunate to be where
i am right now
when i see her
on the lawn swing
in the middle of the yard
one leg extended
the other bent
wearing white shorts riding
high on her soft thighs
a sleeveless top exposing
her graceful arms
as if posing for
a WWII pin up

tossing her head back
she flashes me her
alluring smile
points at me
whispers "come here"

our foreplay is electric
like the air around us

our lovemaking becomes the
quiet moment before
lightning strikes

". . .SO EASY TO BE A POET/. . .SO HARD TO BE/A MAN"

FROM *40,000 FLIES* - CHARLES BUKOWKSI

late sunday night
i knew i was in trouble when my ex called
loud sad mexican songs and drunk people
yelling in the background
i can smell the cuervo on her
breath from 1300 miles away
before i can say hello
she jabs the word "asshole"
into my gut like a hot switchblade
she's just buried her father
and i know from personal experience
how a death can peel back the skin
expose those forgotten scars
and festering wounds from
another time and place

her words flew by like dirty panties
packed with rocks
i heard it all
self centered/selfish/righteous
uncaring/indignant/shameless
ungrateful/sonuvabitch

it's been awhile since i've had
the mirror held this close to my face
and i'll be the first to agree we
all need this from time to time

i almost hang up but tell
myself to be quiet and listen
it's gonna be a late night
monday morning is going
to be a bitch

but for now just
say i'm sorry
and mean it

THE WOMEN AT C.J.'S

it's always a sobering thought
to realize the music i listened to
when i was a punk doesn't even
qualify as oldie-but-goodie
but is more like jurassic park

i'm thinking about leaving
going to another bar with
a kick ass jukebox instead
of a cover band singing
"like a rolling stone" while
high on geritol and shots
of rot gut tequila

when i see them sitting
on the other side of the bar
two middle aged women
one in a pink sweater
hair short and sassy
the type i'd eventually
ask to go steady
sitting with her blonde
cheerleader friend who
wore tight skirts in class
and jumped in the backseat
at the drive-in without
being asked twice

but it's different now
they're hard and lean
bitter around the eyes
maybe a son in college who
has decided to chuck pre-law
and become a poet
maybe a daughter in high
school on the pill

maybe 2 or 3 divorces
to my one

glancing my way
i feel their search through
the pockets of my soul
looking for what i've got to
bring to the table
i feel violated
like having my underwear
drawer ransacked

it's all too much
i decide to down my beer
and make my exit

then miss pink sweater
unwraps a piece
of juicy fruit
pops it into
her pretty mouth
begins chewing the impatient
chew i've seen a
thousand times since jr. high
the chew that says
"you gonna sit there all night
talking to yourself?"

and just like that
nothing else
matters

some of them have been studying us
for many years
in awe of the way we go about
picking the carcass of our planet
like hordes of crabs on a beached whale

they were having a hard time
telling us apart
yeah, we come in different colors
and sizes but for the most part
we all looked alike to them

try it sometime...
watch ants scurrying about
their business
see what i mean?

so it was considered a stroke
of genius when one of the aliens
figured a way to identify us as individuals
while observing the humans of the
american midwest variety it was
determined that every one of us
has a different butt
no two pair of buns are alike
they photograph and catalogue us
according to wrinkles under the cheeks
bumpy jiggly cellulite surfaces
skin tight and hard
hairy or smooth
sticking out or
spread wide

the aliens have even made
our derrieres an industry
on their planet
selling coffee mugs
key chains and beautiful
lifesize posters of various
butts in natural settings

in skin-tight levi's
sitting on a barstool
in New Mexico
or hanging out a window
bare naked from a car
speeding down PCH

no alien's home would
be complete without their
famous artist's painting of
five human hineys
playing poker

so the next time you're walking
down the street or in the mall
and you feel their eyes on you
give it an exaggerated wriggle
then look over your shoulder
flash 'em a knowing wink
and a smile

then dive back into the crowd
hear them gasp in awe admiring
the gift of your elusive beauty
your gentle grace

FRIENDS II

they lived in B.F.E., Indiana
where there was no need for fences
the fields provided all the barriers
needed between neighbors
Mattie was 80 Kate was 76
and they were inseparable
Mattie drove one of those land yachts from the '70's
the ones that got 7 miles to the gallon but could hit
zero to sixty in the blink of an eye
she took Kate everywhere with her
to church, the supermarket, to get their hair done
Mattie couldn't hear and Kate couldn't see
so they complemented each other pretty well
till one day upon returning home from
a trip to the market Mattie was dropping Kate off
and forgot that Kate had to get her stuff out of the backseat
so while she was getting her groceries
Mattie stepped on it, dragging Kate under the tires
of her semi-tank, then she backed up over her friend
as she did a u-turn on the dirt road in a hurry to get
home and see Regis and Kathie Lee

the local pastor was called by the police
to approach the lady and inform her of what
she had done
they say she cried alot
gave up the keys to her car
and now stares out the window
refusing to go anywhere
at all

THE PRESIDENT SIGNS A NEW BANKRUPTCY LAW

meanwhile i'm
down to my last 20 bucks
'til payday and i allot it
accordingly to life's priorities
a 12 pack of Tecate on sale
for 8.99
a pkg of weiners
a pkg of buns
and a bag of doritos

i got a couple
of dollars left
for a rainy day or
to put towards
my retirement

this is my economic
reality

the next day i read
an article on the internet
about hot dogs being a
link to pancreatic cancer

Mr President
in lieu of this new information
and considering all the weenies
i've had to eat lately
you and Bank of America
can kiss my ass

SUPPORTING THE TROOPS

from the bowels of the
planet we suck dry the
slick black liquid that
keeps us humming
along

send our sons and
daughters to faraway
lands to suffer loss
of limb and life to
secure a neverending
supply

we place yellow ribbon
magnets on the backsides
of our suvs to show our
gratitude and continue
to vote like jackasses
blinded by the sun

soldiers dodging bullets
know the real score
wonder what the fuck
they're dying for

it's the annual "let's-see-how-
these-guys-play-war" evaluation
and we're getting our tactical asses
kicked up and down Ft. Carson
making us take a good long look
at the officer in charge

he's feeling the heat
but like every rookie coach
in the playoffs for the 1st time
he's favored by Vegas to call at
least one real boner
so when he lays out the last
battle plan it's a poet's wet dream
a cross between "Custer's Last Stand"
and "the Charge of the Light Brigade"

we all stand back
a shared glance confirming
our common agreement

for his going away present
we all chipped in and gave
him a nickel plated .45
and a bullet engraved
with his initials

FIRST KISS, 8TH GRADE, DEC. 1968

then,
it was this skinny broad cornering me
under some mistletoe,
wrapping her Olive Oyl arms around me, working
her tongue into my mouth like some sort
of persistent key.

and now,
it was the firmness of those
two small breasts pressed against my chest,
the smell of her mother's most expensive perfume,
her soft and wet tongue sliding against my teeth,
my jaws melting like hot wax.

But we did

make love in the light just once
it was our first 4th of July together
i was home alone so you picked me up
stood there in the doorway of the bathroom
watching me, shirtless, as i shaved
before we knew it we were in the
hallway in each other's arms looking
for a soft place to land

it was all a blur except for the graceful
way you extended your muscular calf
and nonchalantly flipped your ankle
sending your underwear delicately flying
across the living room

that night on the beach
your mother's suspicious looks
shot my way like a flurry of
bottle rockets while you
snuggled my head on your lap
stroked my hair
we watched one of the better displays
of fireworks i have ever seen
knowing even though it wasn't as bright
or quite as noisy
we had been there

and done that

On the Outside

it's a mystery to me
how i have so little
in common with my generation
no kids to put through college
no nest egg padded with soft
dreams of condos in Florida
or rustic cabins hidden deep in
the Wisconsin woods

they collect hot stocks
acquire their paper wealth
while i seek out books of poetry
search used cd stores for
vintage jazz classics
they talk about the state of
their current marriage
define themselves around soccer
schedules and seeing the latest
Disney flick

watching them become their parents
i can't help but feel i screwed up
took a left when i should have taken a right
fated to always be on
the perimeter feeling awkward
and undeveloped

but nights when i'm up 'til the wee
hours chasing the perfect poem
can feel its steamy heat brush my cheek
or when i wake up beside a beautiful woman
her gentle snore music to my ears

then it all makes sense and
i give praise to the gods

who took a liking to me
singled me out
pointed me in the direction
i was meant to take

HOW I BECAME HE-WEEPS-FIRE

I.
my post as imperial master
of night sky pictures goes back to when
i was a young man practicing my art
many said i was gifted
kissed as a child by the
venerated dragons of my ancestors
i could make a celestial canvas
black as octopus ink
light up like a thousand suns
the people loved my loud pictures
that moved and shook the walls
of the city when they exploded above

one night i showed off my
latest masterpiece
it was Bu-tan the oxen
everyone recognized him
smiled in delight as the sparks
and smoke shot out from his
flared nostrils
the thunder of the shells
rumbled through the air
many said it felt as if the beast
was actually storming the streets
and alleys

my Lord and Master
Little Storm
was only five years old then
but has often told me
on that night he knew our karma
was one
the next day i was summoned to the palace
became a member of his court

every year on my Master's birthday
i would take him up into the hills
away from the city
put on a show only for his eyes
(really... the guards had to turn
their backs and look down on the ground)
he always saw my best work first
and no matter how old he was
my sky paintings always took him back
to that mystical moment when a man
realizes some things are more important
than he will ever be
his lovely slanted eyes opened wide
pink lips shaped in a delicate "O"
soft hands clapping with each burst
of blinding light
i knew i would be with him forever

II.
in the year 7 White Swan
my Lord assumed the duties of
all powerful and benevolent ruler
he celebrated by leading an army
to the north to subdue those known
only as the barbarians-who-eat-their-
own-shit

his many victories kept me busy
i had to keep the skies
over our land filled with battle scenes
as depicted by his messengers
the people especially cheered
my version of Little Storm's javelin
projected across a starry sea of night
only to explode the head of the fierce
but stupid Asshole-Breath
leader of our new sworn enemies

my Lord defeated many armies
added riches and land to the empire
was away for many years at a time
so when his beautiful wife
my Lady Lotus-Petal began
visiting my studio to watch me work
i did whatever i was asked
quenching the thirst of her loneliness

on her birthday i created what i
considered my greatest masterpiece
to bring her honor and joy
i exploded a lotus of gunpowder and fire
the size of the moon... unfolding itself over
and over in the cool autumn night
while a river of sparks fell
gently like snow flakes from the center
and just as it seemed like
the blossoming had ended
the people were shaken by the thunderous
BOOM! and it would start all over again
my tribute lasted for over an hour
when it was finished
the sound of couples hurrying home
to recreate their own unfolding of the flower
gave the palace historians reason to
dub that night
the-time-of-many-moans

no one knew my Lord
was just outside the city gates
days ahead of his returning army
anxious to surprise Lady Lotus-Petal
later he would tell me as he watched
my display he cried for the beauty
of what it was
and how i could possibly
know it so well

as i was held down by the guards
the hot coals brushing briefly
across my eyes
i heard my Lord's voice tell me
our Lady's last breath
carried my name up to the heavens

Little Storm is most wise
he let me live
continue to work
my destiny to always see darkness
the eternal black canvas i can
never change

when i hear the crowd
ohh and ahh
the children squeal with delight
i can only cry
feel my tears falling
like the hot rain
i create so well

ANOTHER NATURE POEM

sitting at the bar
in Kelly's realizing
i'm 15 minutes away
from being stood up
when the cute redhead
across from me drinking
with her two gay guy pals
turns to slide off her stool
flashing me a glimpse of
her pink undies riding
high above the waist of
her low cut denims
but the back of the chair
has wood curving up
like a pair of dull horns
and one of them ends up
hooking the band of material
from her thong underwear
that rests in the crack of
her ass giving her what I
can only perceive as one
hell of a wedgie
i sit there watching her
struggle and realize i'm
the only one who notices

i want to reach over like
her knight in shining armor
say "allow me" and gently
practice some catch and release
when she finally wriggles her
butt frantically the way a
salmon shakes her tail

swimming upstream to
spawn and frees herself
to go pee

one class act deserves
another so when it was
clear my date was a no-show
i bought the bar a round

AND YET, ANOTHER NATURE POEM

maybe it's me
but when sticking something
up my ass i like to know
what are the ingredients
so imagine my surprise
when flipping over the box
of Preparation H and reading
that it consists of 3% shark
liver oil

it's one thing to end up
fillet'd on some celebrity chef's
cooking show who screams
BAM as he orgasmically rubs
you down with rich aromatic
spices

there are worse ways to go
if you know what i mean
like being hunted down
chopped up and processed
as vital organs are wrung and
squeezed for the precious oils
coveted for the relief they provide
a baby boomer's itchy anal orifice

so the next time you're
on a cruise
riding the glassy surface of
a calm, romantic sea under
a full bahaman or mexican moon
holding your significant other's
hand as you snuggle on deck

making one of those memories
that will give you comfort in
your old age -

at the same moment just a
few feet below the surface
like a pack of nazi submarines
waiting for the right moment
to strike

they are watching
waiting for you to fall in
don't flatter yourself
you don't taste good
for them it's the practical
thing to do
ripping you apart
accomplishes a simple
but vital objective

making sure they have
one less asshole
in the world to
worry about

Upon Receiving a Letter from Hugh Hefner Expressing His Disappointment I'm Letting My Subscription Lapse

Hugh, while i used to covet your interviews
with guys like Miles Davis and Ralph Nader
these days i find myself not giving a rat's ass
what the rapper of the month thinks or
reading about Ben Affleck's personal
reaction upon using viagra
for the first time
and at this stage of my life
when i think of all the women
who shared my bed
i have to say i never slept with one
who came close to looking like
the ladies who grace your pages
their breasts didn't look or feel
like medicine balls
but were soft
bounced and swayed like fruit
in varied degrees of ripeness
and since any year i make 20 grand
is a good year for me
(which explains these 4 yr old jeans i'm wearing)
i think it's obvious i'll never
be able to afford the cars
or threads required to catch
the fancy of your beauties

Hugh, if your life is a sirloin
then mine is a quarter pounder
with cheese

and i can live with that
just fine

TRUER WORDS...

i'm at the Sports Page
on a Friday night
cutting loose with
some co-workers
find the nerve to break
the ice with a curvy blonde
smelling like Winston Lights
and Budweiser
she declines a dance
because she's been moving
all day into her new place
says it took a
lot out of her
uh huh whatever

but it looks promising
so before i offer to buy
a round i go to the john
with thoughts of
maybe
possible
why not
and while standing
in front of the urinal
i look up and read these
words written on the wall
at exactly eye level
as if they had been put there
just for me to see at this
crucial moment in my life:

"no matter how beautiful
she is
someone
somewhere is

sick and tired
of her shit"

pulling up my zipper
i wash my hands
head back into the crowd
remember how the gods
work and why

BABY BROTHER'S SONG OF REDEMPTION

his eyes open everyday
to epiphanies in the polluted
skies over San Gabriel Valley with
a mexican restaurant on every corner and
where high speed chases on the 605 fwy
lead to jobs paying just
enough to stay alive

he learned the hard way
to let go is an act of survival
bitter feelings should be plucked
and discarded like the weeds
choking the flowers we try to grow
in the gardens of our hearts

now he walks in grace among
the winos and meth heads
in peace with the homeless
prophets shouting their visions
of doom and salvation
the rage has subsided from
a fire out of control to the
flame of a single candle

early morning he slips
outside to the smell of
dew on summer grass
the sound of sparrow
singing thanks and praise
as a multitude of blue collar
angels rise to greet the day

standing there, alone
as God speaks his
mind for all to hear

baby brother
my enlightened one
has learned to tune in

Whimper... for Allen Ginsberg

I.
i have seen the best of my generation
selling out for a pittance of what they are worth pursuing
nike commercials and the cover of people magazine
voting for bad actors and heartless economics brutalizing
third world children so we can get a price break on denim jeans
wandering the streets avoiding eye contact avoiding touch avoiding
one another as killer STDs turn desires and needs
from spin the bottle to russian roulette
denouncing inner city crack heads and trailer park chemists caught on
law enforcement reality shows that are watched from the safety of
the homes of boob tube junkies
spending borrowed money to launch angelic armies of death
across the desert and posing prisoners in naked piles of flesh
for cell phone camera feeding frenzies
raping the forests and leaving them bruised and limp for all
to see while jerking off into ponds populated by three legged frogs
sentencing our youth to mtv lobotomy drive-by paranoias and
indentured servitude to the world banks who loan us money today
to pay off the loans of tomorrow
paying compassionate doctors to suck the fat from our hips and
inject it into our lips while burning naked under deadly solar rays trying
to look like a piece of well done meat
digging deep holes to bury atomic poisons lasting a zillion years
and hot dogs that do not decompose
filling space with satellites spying on us so government employees
looking for terrorists can watch us fuck in our bedrooms and count
how many times we say "i love you."

II.
america, we worship at the altar of Rumsfeld and burn the bones of the
dead like sticks of holy incense
america, Rumsfeld is the corporation buying votes to defeat raising
the minimum wage so the working poor will huddle in wal-mart

parking lots waiting for the doors to open
Rumsfeld! Rumsfeld's disney CEOs imprint our children with
moralistic cartoons tied in with cheap plastic action figures and
600 calorie kiddie cheesburgers
Rumsfeld is marketing genius convincing us a sneaker is
not just a sneaker
Rumsfeld is internet porn the new opiate of the people
Rumsfeld! skews his face up in contempt as young american
soldier asks for body armor to keep his nuts from being blown off
america, Rumsfeld embraces defenseless developing nations like
a drunk uncle at a family wedding who tries to slip you the tongue
Rumsfeld is our wall street global terrorist mentality our dreams to
control the markets of the world
Rumsfeld fucks america for not being able to come together for
being split divided conquered controlled me first i got mine
get yours

III.
you are gone
a soul one with
the cosmos of
Christ and Buddha
Krishna Torah and Koran
universal one
accept this
small tribute

from one lacking
the spiritual balls
to howl as loudly
as you